MACMILLAN GUIDE
BEGINNER LI

ELIZABETH LAIRD
The Garden

MACMILLAN GUIDED READERS • ORIGINALS

BEGINNER LEVEL

Founding Editor: John Milne

Macmillan Guided Readers provide a choice of enjoyable reading material for all learners of English. The series comprises three categories: MODERNS, CLASSICS and ORIGINALS. Macmillan **Originals** are specially written stories, published at five levels of grading – Starter, Beginner, Elementary, Intermediate and Upper. At **Beginner Level**, the control of content and language has the following main features:

Information Control

The stories are written in a fluent and pleasing style with straightforward plots and a restricted number of main characters. Cultural background is made explicit through both words and illustrations. Information which is vital to the story is clearly presented and repeated where necessary.

Structure Control

Special care is taken with sentence length. Most sentences contain only one clause, though compound sentences are used occasionally with the clauses joined by the conjunctions 'and', 'but' and 'or'. The use of these compound sentences gives the text balance and rhythm. The use of Past Simple and Past Continuous Tenses is permitted as these are the basic tenses used in narration and students must become familiar with these as they continue to extend and develop their reading ability.

Vocabulary Control

At **Beginner Level** there is a controlled vocabulary of approximately 600 basic words, so that students with a basic knowledge of English will be able to read with understanding and enjoyment. Help is also given in the form of vivid illustrations which are closely related to the text.

For further information on the full selection of titles in all of the categories at every level of the series, please refer to the Readers catalogue.

It was six o'clock. I was tired. It was time to go home. I did not like my work in the shop. I often had headaches and my feet were always tired.

The streets were hot and busy. Everybody was going home. Their faces looked sad.

I passed a flower shop. It was dark and quiet. The flowers smelled sweet and their leaves were wet. I stopped. I looked in my purse. I had a little money. I went into the shop and bought a bunch of flowers.

At home, I put the flowers in a vase. They looked beautiful. I put the vase on the table. I began to make supper. My father came in.

'Where's my food?' he said.

'Nearly ready, Father,' I said.

He picked up a bottle of whisky. He poured some into a glass. The bottle was nearly empty.

'Give me some money, girl,' he said. 'I need some more whisky.'

'You don't need any more,' I said. 'Please, Father, don't buy any more.'

'Shut up, and give me some money,' he said.

'I haven't got any,' I said.

My father was angry. He began to shout at me. He pointed to the flowers.

'You spend money on flowers,' he said. He picked up the vase, and threw it on the floor. The vase broke.

My father went out and shut the door with a bang.

He will get money from a friend, I thought. He will come home drunk again tonight.

I picked up the broken flowers and threw them away. Somebody knocked at the door. I did not want to open it.

It isn't a friend, I thought. Nobody comes here now.

The person knocked again and called my name. I opened the door. It was the old man from next door.

'Come in, George,' I said.

Old George came in and sat down.

'I heard your father,' he said. 'You poor girl. Can I help you?'

I wanted to talk to Old George.

'What can I do?' I said. 'Father drinks whisky all the time. He hasn't got a job. He takes all my money and spends it on drink. Today I bought some flowers. He was angry. He broke the vase. Sometimes I hate him!'

'Do you like flowers?' asked Old George.

'I love them,' I said. 'But they cost a lot of money.'

'Why don't you grow some on your balcony?'

'Grow flowers?' I asked.

'I'll show you,' said Old George. 'I was a gardener once.'

The next day I came home quickly from work. George was waiting outside his flat.

'Come and see,' he said.

I went inside the old man's flat. He had some flower pots and some packets of seeds.

George and I carried the flower pots into my flat. We filled them with earth and planted the seeds. We put the pots on the balcony.

Every evening George and I worked in our balcony garden. George taught me a lot about flowers. He talked about different flowers, about their colour and beauty.

I was happy in my garden. I forgot about my father and my hard work at the shop. George was my friend. I was not lonely any more.

Months passed. My garden became larger and more beautiful. The flowers opened.

My father never came onto the balcony. He did not like flowers. He did not like George. My father was drinking all the time. He always asked me for money and he often hit me. He looked ill.

George was ill too. He coughed and coughed. He was thin and weak. Sometimes he did not come to our garden. He did not leave his bed.

One day, I cooked some food and took it to George. He was lying in bed. He did not turn and smile at me. He did not move.

I went closer to him. His eyes were open. I touched his hand. It was cold. He was dead.

I went back to our flat. My father was there. He was waiting for his supper.

'George is dead,' I said. I began to cry. 'He was kind to me. I will miss him.'

My father looked at me, but he said nothing. He took some money and went out of the house.

My father came home late that night.

'Why are you crying?' he said. 'Are you crying for George? You loved that silly old man, didn't you? What about me? I'm your father. You don't care about me.'

I said nothing. My father began to shout.

'I've got a surprise for you, my girl. A nice young man. What do you think of that? He's a good boy. He's a friend of mine. You need a man, not a garden.'

I stared at my father. I said nothing.

'Look at yourself,' my father said. 'You're not pretty, and you're getting old. Nobody else will marry you.'

'No, Father, no!' I said. 'I'm not going to marry anybody. I'm staying here. I don't want to leave my garden.'

'Your garden, your garden!' my father shouted. 'Your silly garden! You spend all your money on plants. You never give me money. You don't talk to me. You talked to Old George. I hated him. And I hate your garden.'

I ran away from my father. I went to my bedroom and locked the door.

There was a lot of noise. My father was shouting and breaking things. After a long time, the noise stopped.

I left my bedroom and went to the balcony. The balcony door was open. I looked out. The pots were broken and the plants were torn to pieces. The garden was ruined.

I went to my father's room.

I hate him, I said to myself. I'll tell him. He can kill me. I don't care.

My father's door was locked. I banged and shouted. He did not open it. He did not hear me. He was asleep. He was drunk.

I went back to my room.

What shall I do? I thought. Where shall I go?

I looked round the room. I took some clothes and packed them in a bag. I found some packets of flower seeds and put them in the bag. Then I took my purse and counted my money. I did not have very much.

I left the flat and shut the door quietly. I stood outside George's door for a minute. I wanted to say goodbye.

It was dark outside. The roads were empty. There were no cars or people. It was very late.

I must leave the town, I said to myself. I must go to the country. Perhaps I can work in a garden.

Some hours later, morning came. People were going to work. There were some cars on the road. A bus came along. It stopped near me. I climbed onto it.

On the bus, I fell asleep. Then somebody touched my arm. I woke up.

'The bus stops here,' a man said. 'You must get off.'

I got off the bus and looked round. I was in a small village. The town was far away.

I was hungry. I went to a café and sat down. I bought some bread and tea. Now I had very little money.

I must find work, I thought.

I spoke to the waiter.

'Can you help me?' I asked him. 'I don't know this place. I need work. I can work as a gardener. Who can give me a job?'

The waiter thought for a moment.

'There's Mrs Jack,' he said. 'She's got a market garden. Perhaps she can help you.'

Mrs Jack's market garden was two miles away. I was very tired, but I walked fast.

The garden was on the side of a hill. There was a notice over the gate:

JACK'S GARDEN
Fresh vegetables and fruit for sale

I stood at the gate and looked inside. I saw a long line of greenhouses and a field of fruit trees. There was a small house behind the field. I liked the place.

A woman came out of the house. She saw me at the gate and came up to me.

'Who are you?' she said. 'What do you want?'

'Can you give me a job?' I asked.

'No work here,' said the woman. She turned and walked away. Suddenly she stopped and came back.

'Wait a minute,' she said. 'We have a new greenhouse. I'll need some help. Come with me.'

I followed Mrs Jack to the house. She asked me many questions about plants and gardening. I knew the answers. Old George was a good teacher.

'I'll give you a job,' said Mrs Jack. 'You can start today.' She smiled for the first time.

Mrs Jack gave me a room in her house. I worked hard for her, and I loved the work. I liked the country. I liked the fresh air and the sunshine. I did not think about my father. But I often thought about George.

Mrs Jack was kind. She paid me well for my work and gave me good food. But I did not like her son, Harry. He was a big man, with thick glasses. He did not talk much or smile. He watched me all the time. His eyes followed me.

One day I was working in the new greenhouse. I was watering the tomatoes.

I'm safe here, I thought to myself. I'm far away from my father and his friend.

I heard somebody behind me. I turned round. It was Harry. He took my hand and smiled at me.

'I like you,' he said. 'You're a nice girl.'

I pushed Harry away.

'Go away!' I said. 'Don't touch me! I hate men. You are all the same. You drink, and fight, and break things. Leave me alone.'

I ran out of the greenhouse. I wanted to be alone.

After that day, Harry did not look at me. He did not speak to me. I was glad.

One day I had an idea.

I need my own little garden, I thought. I'll grow some flowers. Then I will forget about Father and Harry. I'll make something beautiful.

There was a small piece of ground near the house. I pulled out the weeds and dug the earth. I had George's packet of flower seeds. I planted them in my new garden and watched them grow.

My new garden grew well. The flowers had beautiful colours. They smelt sweet. One day, Mrs Jack visited my garden.

'Look, Mrs Jack,' I said. 'Flowers grow well here. Why don't we grow some in the market garden? You sell fruit and vegetables. We can sell flowers too. You can make more money.'

'That's a good idea,' Mrs Jack said. 'It's your idea, and you can do the work. But where will you sell the flowers? There's no flower shop here.'

I remembered the flower shop in the city. It was near my father's flat. I bought my first bunch of flowers in that shop.

Next day I got up early. I picked some of my best flowers. I took the bus to the city.

In the city the streets were hot. The people looked tired.

Life is better in the country, I thought. The people in the country are happier.

I walked quickly to the flower shop. I looked round all the time. I did not want to meet my father.

The people in the shop were friendly.

'Yes, we'll buy your flowers,' said the manager. 'They are very, very beautiful.'

I was pleased. I thought of Mrs Jack and my garden in the country. I wanted to go back at once. I left the shop and began to walk quickly.

On the corner of the street, there was a beggar. He was old and very thin. His clothes were dirty. He had dirty hair and red eyes. He put out his hand.

'Help me, lady,' he said. 'Help a poor old man.'

I knew his voice. I looked at him. It was my father.

I wanted to run away. I wanted to go back to the country and forget my father for ever. But I stood still. I felt sorry for him.

'Father?' I said.

His old, red eyes looked up. There were tears in them. He knew me.

'It's you?' he said.

'What happened to you, Father?' I asked.

'You ran away,' he said. 'You left me. I was ill for a long time. I was lonely without you. I was a bad father, but you were always a good daughter. You worked hard. I took all your money and sometimes I hit you. I broke up your garden. I . . .'

'Don't talk about it, Father,' I said.

'I wanted to buy whisky,' he said, 'but I didn't have any money. My friends left me. They didn't want me any more. Now I'm a lonely old man. I stand here and beg. Sometimes people give me a little money. I get a little food. I sold the furniture in the flat. But I kept your things for you.'

I thought again of my new life in the country. I felt all round me the sadness of the city. I took my father's arm.

'Come on, Father,' I said. 'We're going home.'

There was not much furniture in the flat. There were dirty cups and plates in the kitchen. There was a bad smell of dirt and old food. I looked round sadly. My father saw my face.

'Everything is dirty,' he said. 'I can't clean the flat. You made everything nice. I needed you here.'

I did not say anything. I went to my room. Everything was the same. I thought of my last night at home. It was a long time ago. I went back to my father. I began to clean the flat.

The next day I wrote a letter to Mrs Jack. I told her everything.

'I am sorry. I cannot work for you any more,' I wrote. 'I must stay here and look after my father.'

I began my old life once more. I took my old job again. I came home every evening and cooked for my father. I did not make my garden again. I felt too sad.

My father was very different now. He did not drink any more. He looked much older. He talked to me kindly. But he lived in the past. Sometimes he talked to my mother. But my mother was dead. She died a long time ago.

One evening, somebody knocked on the door. I opened it. It was Mrs Jack's son, Harry. He was holding a large bunch of flowers. They were flowers from my little garden in the country.

'We're selling flowers to the flower shop now,' he said. 'I bring them to the city every week. But these are for you.'

He gave me the flowers and left quickly.

The flowers were beautiful.

I'll make my balcony garden again, I thought.

I worked on my garden every evening. Soon, flowers began to grow on the balcony again. My father liked the garden. He sat all day on the balcony. Sometimes he slept. Sometimes he talked to himself.

Harry came every week and brought me flowers. He never spoke. He gave me the flowers and went away.

'Come in and have a cup of tea, Harry,' I said one day. He came in and sat down quietly.

'Come and see my balcony garden,' I said.

My father was sitting on the balcony. Harry sat down beside him. I went to the kitchen and made some tea. I heard their voices. They were laughing. I was happy.

The old man needs a friend, I thought.

Harry was kind to my father. They talked and laughed. I watched them.

I was wrong about Harry, I thought. He is kind and gentle.

Every week, Harry came to the flat. He and my father became friends. My father loved his visits.

I often looked at Harry. Behind the thick glasses, his eyes were kind and gentle. He often smiled now.

I saw other things, too. I saw his kindness to my father. I saw his love for flowers.

One day, I was watering the plants in my balcony garden. My father was asleep in the sun. Harry came up to me. He put his arms round me.

'I want to ask you something,' he said.

'Yes, Harry,' I said, 'I'm listening.'

But Harry said nothing. I looked at his eyes. I understood.

'It's all right, Harry,' I said. 'The answer is "yes".'

Published by Macmillan Heinemann ELT
Between Towns Road, Oxford, OX4 3PP
Macmillan Heinemann ELT is an imprint of
Macmillan Publishers Limited
Companies and representatives throughout the world

ISBN 0 435 27172 5

Text © Elizabeth Laird 1979, 1992, 1998, 2002

First published 1979
Design and illustration © Macmillan Publishers Limited 1998, 2002
Heinemann is a registered trademark of Reed Educational and Professional Publishing Limited
This version first published 2002

All rights reserved; no part of this publication may be
reproduced, stored in a retrieval system, transmitted in any
form, or by any means, electronic, mechanical, photocopying,
recording, or otherwise, without the prior written permission of
the publishers.

Illustrated by Irene Wise
Cover by Faranak and Threefold Design

Printed in China

2006 2005 2004 2003
15 14 13 12 11 10 9 8